Unexpected

poetry by
Martin Willitts Jr.

Unexpected
>Paperback Edition, perfect bound, laminated 90# cover, printed on 50# crème paper and set in Dolly Pro type.

ISBN: 978-1-943900-07-7
Library of Congress Control Number: 2019953255

Manufactured and distributed worldwide by the Ingram Book Company. Produced, published and marketed by Duck Lake Books, Ocean Shores, Washington, U.S.A.

cover art: *Dandelion Sun*
Adina Voicu, 2018

Duck Lake Books
www.ducklakebooks.com

Acknowledgments:

I would like to thank the following publications where many of these poems appeared, often in a different version:

Adelaide Literary Journal: "How Could We Not Know Winter is Near," "Love is Never Far from Us"

Alexandria Quarterly: "Clouds"

The Aurorean: "Laundry Hanging Day," "Planting," "The Weather is About to Break"

Big River Poetry Review: "Opus 18"

Black Poppy Review: "Rain"

Border Crossing: "This is Why I Plant Perennials"

Broadkill River Review: "Afternoon Rain," "In the Dark Violence"

Caesura: "Gratefulness"

Califragile: "Unexpected," "Winter Wind"

Comstock Review: "The Distant Calling," "Opus 22"

Cloudburst Anthology: "Tender Moments"

Duck Lake Journal: "Music," "Raining on a Pond"

Evening Street Review: "Coming Home, Soon"

Kentucky Review: "Opus 9"

Moon Magazine: "Opus 15"

Night Garden Journal: "The Song"

Page & Spine: "Opus 2", "Opus 4," "Opus 10," "Opus 11"

Poetry Matters Project (Finalist): "Different Kinds of Light During a Snowstorm"

Poppy Road Review: "Opus 13," "Opus 14," "Whatever We Are Doing in Life"

Quiet Storm: "After Winter"

Seven Circles Press: "Opus 5," "Opus 20"

Shelia-Na-Gig: "But, Boy, what a Day it Has Been"

Turtle Island Quarterly: "Grasshopper's Song," "The Release from Forever"

Verse-Virtual: "Just Now," "Light Breaking Clouds," "Never Easy," "Not Geese"

Zingara (*"Poetry Pick of the Week"*): "Stillness"

"Mallards: and "The Sunflower" appeared in the anthology, *Like Light: 25 Years of Poetry and Prose* (Bright Hill Press, 2018

"Opus 1," "Opus 6," "Opus 8," "Opus12," "Opus17," "Opus 16," "Opus 17," "Opus 19," "Opus 21," "Opus 23", "Opus 24" appeared in the chaplet *Opus Poems*, (*Black Poppy Review*, 2016)

"Opus 7" appear as "First Love is Best Love" in the anthology. *Love Notes* (*Vagabond Press* anthology, 2012)

Contents

Part I

Part III

Unexpected

Part I

Planting

I kneel in front of the dark earth as rain molds to me.
My fingers probe gently to find that sacred place
where life begins.
This offering is such a small seed.
The sun breaks free of the clouds.
I part the mound, thrust the seed in, gently.

I have tended to this planting like playing music.
Life begins this simply, this lightly, this lovingly.
Everywhere is murmuring with pleasure. I leave
the garden, enter my house, hold my wife like rain.

The Song

I love you as much as air.
What have I done to deserve you?
I'm almost exhausted
by the absoluteness of love.

Even in the quiet garden
planting gardenias, I hear you,
singing a summer rain.
What have I done to deserve you?

My joy is almost crippling
with an ache for more.
I notice moisture in the rain.
Drops hang in air,

tiny bells trying to ring.
I am constantly lighthearted,
dizzy with hypnotic love.
My face is a song of rain;

a song arriving from you
moves the metronome
of my heart, opening
into a white gardenia.

The Grasshopper's Song

A grasshopper was bringing music,
but I wasn't listening.

Instead, I heard the lament of someone
in anguish, almost begging to be understood,
insisting, *You never loved me.* It chirruped,
Love is such an antique desire.

This is the one song the grasshopper wanted to tell,
to fill to overflowing, but also, it wanted me to empty.
Since I had ignored both messages, the grasshopper
whizzed around me, scolding, *Listen, listen, listen!*

Light was snapping, so I listened
to that exquisite green music.
The song was like smashing pots,
but also, like mending them.

I had to know and understand the difference.
I had to listen closely if I ever expected to learn.
The earth and sky were bearing down on me
all the time, and I never noticed. I wasn't hearing
what they were singing.

They were chanting, *Love me, Love me.*

Laundry Hanging Day

She knows it is probably the last day
to hang laundry, as long as the weather holds.
The season is thinning. The days are colder.
She studies the cloud cover blocking the sun,
willing the clouds out of the way. She pins
hope. The clothes are heavy with water,
so she twists water out. It will have to do.
She is tempting the rain; she knows it,
but it'd be worth it to have pine scent
in the sheets when she goes to sleep.

The fabric will remember the trees
and woodpeckers and the small,
sensitive ferns closing when touched.

She looks to the clouds for a sign,
any sign. Will it rain? Will it clear up?
She tries willing the clouds into moving.
She hums like a bee. She hears her husband
hammering loose shingles before winter sets in.
The wooly bear caterpillar was as fat as her thumb:
a true sign the snow will last as long as her laundry line.

Will the weather hold just a little bit longer?
Geese are spreading sheets in the sky.

Perhaps, the day will remain perfect, just for her:
unspoiled, unsoiled, dry to the touch. Please,
she prays, let something be perfect.

Rain

Listen to the rain's obsession. It's leisurely,
unstoppable remorse. It is squatting over our house.
It runs back and forth like field mice.
It's monotonous.
It cancelled a parade; now, it is cartwheeling
over the fields like a girl in love with a boy
too dumb to know how lucky he can be.
Rain soaks into skin, deep-rooted bliss.

It's steady, heart-throbbing.
Even at dark noon, it bursts open again
and again, not offering reprieve, only revision:
rivulets of mud; sunken cars; drenched
histories; the smell of damp ewes.
A wet monarch clings to a swaying milkweed.

Raining on a Pond

The broad acres are crackling with light
and new feverous life. Rain stretches
over a pond, making xylophone sounds.
Silence and splattered light
settles in our bones, kneels hard
into a shiver not letting go easily.

Mallards

Those teal and striking blue wings
of mallards on the pond
know it is *decision-time:* stay; or go.
There is no in-between. Move on, return;
or weather it out. Stay in the familiar; or
take a high-risk into the unknown.
Float in contentment and serenity,
fully in the Presence; or glide off
into the faraway
where the sun still knows warmth.

They test the winds, ruffle feathers,
notice: the wind has died off,
but the air has a tang, a hint of chill,
an uncomfortable silence
which could bring nothing
or the harshest winter.

Some could stay, some might go:
there is no telling at this point.
Whatever they decide,
will be a solitary decision.

I think of the people I have known
who get this piercing look before dying,
trying to decide to linger;
or praying for a quick, painless end,
heading off into that unknown risk.

This Is Why I Plant Perennials

Every time I plant the perennials —
daffodils, tulips, tiger lilies, hollyhocks —
I'm leaving a part of me immortal:
my immeasurable desire.

I anticipate those first green shoots,
foreshadowing my promise to myself.
Planting is more than peace-filled,
silent meditation, or renewal.

And when flowers die, falling to darkness,
they will not represent eventual revival
or the promise of return, yet their seeds
are reminders of my pledges for more.

More voices, more colors, more for
someone to remember me. People
might continually travel by commenting,
I saw him planting there —

flowers forever arriving on schedule:
daffodils, pink tulips, tiger lilies tasting
sunlight, fifteen-foot hollyhocks
looking over fences for me.

The Sunflower

opens its green fist
one finger at a time
until we witness
all the yellow triangles
surrounding the large brown button of seeds

it remains attentive to the sun for weeks
then slowly curls its yellow triangles
dropping one by one
until all that remains
is the brown center
being eaten by small birds

I had been glancing at pictures of my son
transitioning from infant to adult

I could not see either while they happened
transpiring and conspiring to make me older
under the surface of forever

I am at the summit of time
descending
while the matte finish of my son ascends

I can tell you this
the incline is somehow more straight down vertical
I do not want to let go just yet
any more than that last yellow petal

Clouds

A cloudbank, low to the ground,
was easy to walk through; he did,
entering into the next world.

She tried to follow, but
the secret door had already vanished
into mist, breaking apart.

She had hesitated. The moment went
before she could respond,
and all she could do, was wonder —

what was it like, there? She'd miss him, perhaps;
perhaps not. He had tangible faults,
but he had other qualities she couldn't name,

until later, maybe, maybe when she had time
to reflect, evaluate, and time to sob
clouds of quiet rain. Perhaps then.

Perhaps not even then. Perhaps, never.
She questioned her own tangibility as she, too,
became one with the longitude and latitude

where we could belong, or not.
I'd witnessed her dying, one hour
after her husband, her face no longer clouded.

Coming Home, Soon

Coming home soon, promised the man
in a letter to a woman he'd left behind.

It was with this picture of a man,
still boyishly smiling in an oversized uniform
leaving to fight a war, all fired up,
never thinking he might not return.

They all believed they were bullet-proof,
but some weren't. He wrote: *Coming home, soon.*

Does it matter which war I am talking about,
which side, whose cause? That fling he had
before departing, with a woman he barely knew —
he never thought it would lead to anything,
much less a child. Now, he had to tell her,
he'd marry her when he came back, *soon.*

But he never returned. Maybe, she'd find someone
willing to take her and another man's child.
Someone who wouldn't mind. Someone, hopefully
decent. Someone who would come home.
Someone who would not die in a car accident
or from chain-smoking or a mine collapse.

I found this picture, and a few letters
hidden inside a bureau from an estate sale,
of a man with a sideways, loopy grin,
red-lipped kissed on his cheek
by the woman teasing his hair.

I also found the letter from the government
explaining in blunt terms he never survived.

I had promised my wife I'd be coming home soon,
kissing her to make sure I'd remember
what I had, giving a promise worth keeping.

Just Now

Just now, an ocean wave covers a beach
and retracts,
like a man pacing
while his wife gives birth.

Time is never suspended,
although it might feel that way—
unmoving as everything around it is moving
in contradiction.

We think time evaporates.
Nothing could be further from the truth.
Nor does it move faster forward, accelerating
quicker than we can perceive it.

Just now, a white film of snow is settling
for an indeterminate amount of time,
bringing the premonition of winter.
Otherwise, how else would we know change?

The world has beginnings and absolute endings.
Just now, a meteor has a trajectory across
the universe; a rain drops on water, ripples out,
closing like the valve of a heart.

But, Boy, what a Day it Has Been

A red sky at night — amber flames,
violet clouds — before a starburst
swarm of galaxies is blanketed
and orange sun collapses
below the horizon, hot, torrid,
a calypso dancer snapping fingers.

Crickets escalate their blazing warnings —
sending out their music
drifting like canoes without paddles
or maple leaves scrumming the water surface
with enflamed fingerprints.

Sweat-heavy, breath-laden with moisture
constricting our lungs, we head towards a bed
soaked with the day's perspiration.

Even the slight breeze is humid. But, boy,
what a day it was — waves of light
practically sparkled; sunflowers opened
tentative yawns and the bees found them
tempting; and the clanging of the rope
on the pulley meant relief was rising
to the surface like a halleluiah
when a couple celebrate
their first red-faced bawling baby.

Whatever We Are Doing in Life

Whatever we are doing in life
can't possibly be as important as
what we could be doing.

Stop whatever we are doing. Think:
what good could we be doing;
and, why aren't we doing it?

Days keep floating by.
We can never catch them.
What would we do with them if we could?

All summer, bees are transferring
their loads into heavenly oils.
What have we been doing?

All winter, trees plan new leaves.
The language of love billows on the sky.
What are we doing?

The horizon is rumpling with hills.
Whatever was crazy with business halted,
relaxed its breath to admire what is here.

What is taking us so long?
Go out. Explore what is provided.
There is some for you, some for me.

The Release from Forever

Endless rip tides of clouds are migrating,
untangling from elm trees.

A red-tailed hawk floats in stained glass sky
leaving a trail of rapt quiet, emerging
and vanishing, skimming the sightline.

No noise entered this moment.

I was at the right place, exact time,
to see this release.
Otherwise, there was emptiness to see.

In that quickness,
a pail full of blue spilled onto the sky.

All separation and merging blends fast,
switching between noticed
and gone.

We question: did we see what we think we saw?
Then, the mahogany night fills in all the blank spaces.

The hawk did not even leave smoke when it sealed the sky.
There was no going back to *before.*

Gratefulness

A stream of debris follows a comet
in a hundred and thirty-three-year orbit,
and tonight, I will see the lightshow
through a telescope on a high slope
away from ambient light of city haze.
No one is here with me;

only solitude and clear skies, the pines,
and meteors making their long journey
in that endless heart-stopping arc.

Those particles have been up there
for thousands of years trailing
behind the comet Swift–Tuttle.
And here I am, my eyes following it, too.

It is mid-July, the best time to witness
the shooting stars of the Pleiades shower.
Conditions have to be perfect.
The dark has to be overwhelming,
and cloudless as far as forever.

It's pre-dawn. Meteoroids rise up
by the side of the Earth, speeding forward,
sixty miles per hour, dizzying fireballs.

Afterwards, my heart is still following
as they trail away.

Love Is Never Far from Us

Love, perhaps, is not far from us,
yet it seems so far away;
we are overwhelmed with loss.

When we believe (for our belief is false)
love is gone forever, it betrays —
love, perhaps, is not far from us.

Love is never far away. Love is never lost.
It is with us every day.
We are overwhelmed with loss.

Small moments remind us what's false.
Love comes again, today and today.
Love, perhaps, is not far from us;

maybe, the sadness is just across.
We never know completely what to say,
we are overwhelmed with loss.

We try to hold on and let go at all costs.
Sometimes, love comes unexpectantly.
Love, perhaps, is not far from us —
we are overwhelmed with loss.

Stillness

How do we still the stillness,
making it less than a soft whisper of sleep?
One more day no one can take problems anymore,
and look at how badly it turned out
as the sun sighed, going out
behind the black-purple night sky background.

How can we make it any more quiet
than when the sun is a red flood
disappearing under the weight of the setting
and the pushing down of night?

The large orange harvest moon
sits on the horizon
like it was a hard-wooden park bench.
It is so close we can see the pockmarks
from eons of smashing asteroids,
and we do not know what to say —

how do we get more silence, less
talking, less accidental noises
than that? Less than an oar
not moving in water, not dripping
when lifted, not tipping into the row boat
as it is tied onto a pier, and not
the soundlessness of the wooden dock —
how do we get less noise than that?

Even the moth flaming after touching fire
makes a subtle noise. Or the cat, padding
on a thick rug, clawing and sharpening its nails,
arching before circling into sleep,
makes a curious noise, one that troubles
the quiet. No matter how softly we proceed,
noise follows us, makes sure we know it's there.

Unexpected

Part II

Music

Every day is burnished by sound,
because often, sound remains when the music ends.
Fingers recall each note as they occurred.

When music is necessary and urgent,
invisible and echoing, elemental,
it can be found everywhere —

even in the black-eyed Susan,
even the water searching for the nearest shore.
Every day is burnished by sound.

Preparing for Winter

It rains, cold, damp, fall preparing for winter.
Knowing what to say is more difficult than you might think.
I keep revising. Some words are better than others.

The rain is steady, erasing the day.

Early winter is miserable and punctual.
Snow is blank paper pressing on the ground.
this emergency of writing.

Now it is raining, again.

It is cold. I cannot feel anything,
and whatever I need to say is being revised.

Unexpected

Stubbornness must be that crane
late to leave, trying to push its large body
against strong artic headwinds.
The wings' desire is stronger,
for the crane will find when it lands
another chance to love,
where the sun practically crawls out
of the ocean, and it inquires of the crane,
will you come and join me? And it does —
but not before producing a hatchling
who will learn the art of flying, the art
of spontaneous joy, the touch of excitement.
What appears as containment is really release.

Winter Wind

Contents of snowflakes spill out of her apron pockets.
I have to listen between the snow-dust to hear
whatever she is telling me in her sub-zero breath.
She writes on my window with frost fingerprints,
words crinkling at the edges.

The wind is a cello solo afterwards.

Loss in the Forest of Snow

In whiteness, the most narrowing of light,
birches fade in, reduced to zero.

I could have been circling for hours
like a giant snowy owl.

I do not remember how I came back home —

legs, tired and snow-caked, trudged numbly
even when I arrived at my white door, knocking
like a woodpecker, *Let me in.*

Was that my voice?
It was hollow and wind-broken,
snowflakes flying out of me.

I came out of nothingness;
and I will die into nothingness,

a swirl of snow — nothing more, nothing less.

Different Kinds of Light During Snowstorms

A blinding light bounces off snow,
and people lose sight, crash about
a couple of miles from home.
But the worst accidents tend to be
the ones closest to home.

Other times, snow makes blue light
between a cluster of trees — a peculiar buzz
from the skin of loss. It thrashes,
sleeplessly. No one can comfort it
and it cannot comfort anybody.

Both are roughly spoken consonants.
I barely can speak a warning
when snow absorbs all words.

When a couple argues, I never hear birds sing.
Outside it could be snowing communion wafers;
no one would care.
Snow keeps shoveling in and light is less,
and the pent-up needs release.
Arguments pile into drifts.

I want to lighten this, throw some light on it,
knowing jarring nerves bounce like prism light.
Words are trees behind a screen of blue snow.
No one is comforted by a drift of anger.
Accidents tend to be worse at home.

How Could We Not Know Winter is Near?

Of course, the season grays.
Of course, we came into the weather unprepared.
All danger really ever teaches us
is that nothing is contained or restrained.

Late fall will be nasty, light will dwindle,
and we'll withdraw into our home,
hoping winter will not last forever. Of course,
we doubt it will end anytime soon.

Of course, snow clouds hover.
Light jaunts between snow.
I begin counting every moment until the land vanishes.
Oh course, the cold bites without teeth.

That moan — like a thrash of winter wind —
is my soul. Of course, it is. Of course.
My soul feels gray, unprepared for the long duration.
My soul is seen in my breath in sub-zero air.

Winter Solstice

Winter solstice. Light leaves
using Cooper's hawk wings.
Death speaks the language of raptors.

I walked through snowy fields —
white pine and birch seedlings
laden with snow.

The ground is uneven. Hidden
rocks and tree roots are a maze.
Everywhere has evergreen smell.

At some places, snow deepens
and sighs. It is knee-high,
clinging to pants like burrs.

When I was at a stream,
I could hear it rushing
to get somewhere —

where it is warmer, where
the sun remembers
what it is supposed to do.

And the sun does — it swims out
of the lake into the sky,
shedding snow

like laments; and the snow's scales
are birch bark
in the labyrinth of morning.

After Winter

The weather is breaking,
loosening its grip on the green
under snow. Crocuses are breathing,

sighing, *Where is spring?*
A few signs are being seen —
the weather is breaking;

nubs of first leaves are waking
to see what it all means.
Under snow, crocuses are breathing

green dreams. Father is dying
in a white room behind a screen.
The weather is breaking

across his face, whitening
just before spring seems
under snow. Crocuses are breathing,

purple, living briefly. I'm grieving;
letting him release, a dream
the weather is breaking
under snow. Crocuses are breathing.

Never Easy

Purified snow with glimpses
of deepest-filled land
resumes a blue light
and arrangements of silence.

Hard and cold
intervals of wind move gusts,
making pinwheels of snow.

Never, never, again never, forever,
hammers the heart.
Never, never, someone writes,
sobbing like snow
shaken in a snow globe. Never,
never, rocks the snow
slowing the world to a crawl.

Never, actually never works long.
It is never, never forever, breaking
like sunlight directly on snow,
reflecting blinding light.

Never say never.

I stopped believing in time
healing any wound,
but eventually, it does.

I never minded the break in weather,
or the end of never or forever,
never doubting
completely
change was coming;

but I tried not to count on it,
never believing completely
it was that easy.

The snow had blown
off an icy creek, pockets of ice had broken,
clear water was rushing,
never staying still.

Prediction

Six more weeks of winter cabin fever —
more shovelfuls of greyness, more time
for the desperate sparrows to hope.
I've plunged through the waist-high snow
to fill the feeder and prayed the squirrel
will not tilt the feeder, knocking
the seed everywhere into the whiteness.

Six more weeks of spinning, grinding tires
on roads turned into an ice rink.
Six more shivering weeks of drab
slug-like colored snow. Bad news is counted
by inches of snowfall, dipping temperatures,
plows running all night to keep up.

We keep getting messages, *Soon it will break,
soon we will be complaining about the heat.*
Foolish talk. Six more weeks could last ten.
Snow dangles in the air, tentatively,
too cold to fall.

Whenever there is a moment
of silence and the snow has moved elsewhere,
the sparrows hiding in the thickets
become agitated, excitedly jabbering
about how spring will be coming.

Soon, they promise each other, *Soon*.
Then a blizzard arrives, full-blast,
creating an ebb of disappointment
of sparrows going quiet,
ashamed they were wrong, jumping the gun,
professing such wonderful news —
such false hope and wild speculation.

The Weather is About to Break

The sky is diaphanous. Someone points out the obvious —
what little we have that is permanent. It is never enough.

Unresolved parts from the past extend to the future,
sometimes summoning the worst in us,
turning anger into a blunt instrument.

We hold the emptiness of unfulfilled promises,
unable to move ahead. We question
without receiving answers. Light barely emerges
over the horizon, fleetingly, almost refusing to appear.

We ache for that warmth. It has been a long winter,
and only desire remains, ebbing. Sensing a break,
the hidden birds are chittering, excitedly.

That one sprung-free moment whispers
to ignore those distractions heading our way.
Memory will fiddle around, transcribing and editing,
from second to second, until completely re-arranged.

Tender Moments

There is much to love in this world,
and much I've never seen, but can guess
easily has to be spectacular —

between two large stones and nowhere else,
opening green mouths like fledglings
these tongues of blue-purple violets.

The news occupies itself with danger
and terrible weather and leaders lying
straight-faced. You can have all of that.

A robin touches down, hopping across
the grass, not afraid of me.
This is a tender moment.

If you care to look for these moments,
sense a blush of sunrise; lilacs odors;
rain falling just enough, not more,

not less; a crow cocking its head
suspicious of the silence; or
violets returning every year.

First Light

breaking soil stubborn with hope
what I plant will survive

the day gathers moments
into strings of light

jays are building into a crescendo
assembling a necklace of moments.

Geese Leaving a Lake

There was so much blinding whiteness
heading into the sun, my eyes had an afterglow.

Geese went up — heavy, deliberate,
slow, carrying blueness into the sky,

against gravity, strenuous, pushing hard
against wind resistance,

fighting the urge to quit,
but wanting the sheer responsibility of it,

a communal effort and action,
a rumble of angels.

The geese were rearranging into a pattern,
the air rocking like someone left a hammock.

I had heard that passion could do this.
Now, I had seen it.

They were pointing the way forward
like a Geiger counter responds to the hidden.

The geese were speaking the language of love.
I had heard this, too, was possible.

I watched the geese launch like a Greek armada,
never knowing what was ahead: glory or death.

Everywhere beneath them
was changing,

knowing no one can ever go back
and not be a part of the change.

Unexpected

Part III

Light Breaking Clouds

It is not suddenly a dark cloud lowering
to the lake with precision,
building up, escalating over time.
I watch it form a careful message, knowing
I cannot interrupt this transformation
or change its solemn course.

All I can do is observe
and record as it unfolds, belonging more
to the other world than to this.

I see light penetrating,
breaking the ominous apart, spilling light
in haphazard directions — some for you,
some for me, some for the grateful,
some for the ungrateful.

From the depths of despair,
we can only rise. It is then
I realize this the only life we have —

these few moments are all we are given,
this awesome responsibility
to share these small discoveries
before we forget them.

So, I rush out to tell you, dear one,
to shake you out of a slumber of not-seeing,
to get you to focus, to share,
to see what I am seeing,
to let it sink deep into your memory:

an echo —
like necessary air; like a cloud
reforming at the edge of an iris sunset,
purple and throbbing an excited heart,

recording and looping inside your mind
for days when you might need it.
And light will crack out of you,
this way and that — some for strangers,
some for friends, some for the lost, some
for the people finding their way into light.

Light is Always Present

The day begins and ends with light
followed by birds trying out their songs
in rain or snow.

Working in the garden, I plant light,
water, flowers, soil, hoping light
will accept my offering.

Light follows me to my house,
like visions, like welcomed guests,
like music no one can see.

Light finds the blue clematis,
and the indifferent moths
as they travel from plant to plant.

Light glitters off the rose garden
with trellises arched over sidewalks, and
the daisy almost hiding in the shade.

Light shines on the hopeless romantics
holding hands, with waves of light.
Nothing can avoid light.

There is always some ambient light,
as two lovers try turning off the light
emitting from their glowing bodies.

An Unappeasable Need

after false starts of spring
snow melts briefly
into brown patches
where birds convene

in the return of light
on first piece of green

ravenous blue-black skies
open raven wings
raining streaks of daylight
entangled in branches
with tiny buds waiting
to burst into leaf-songs

a swarm of blackbirds
are a week away from glances
of spring

Practicing Departures

Canada geese are leaving everyone behind
without a hint of what to do next.

Leaves part with wind — some close,
some faraway; some to below where my feet
shuffle like random notes.

I see the future in the entrails of the gut-shot deer
pulling itself through the woods to hide
where hunters cannot find its suffering,
eyes not seeing any more where it is heading.

I cannot stop pain. I do not know how to heal it.

Geese keep trying to exit, flying blindly into head-
winds, into the fading yellow, into the bloody sunset.

Afternoon Rain

It is so quiet, even the steady,
cool rain
wants to nap.

At moments this still,
the room closes its eyes.
Me, too.

Heartbeats and rain
fall together,
in love. Slow

and gentle, easing in
to the other, and now,
silence joins.

Even the nap goes silent.
Sound drifts off. It is quiet,
raining.

Forget About the Boat Swollen with Water

water will take the innocent
and the unwelcomed
equally
into the blue endless horizon
where no one will remember them

forget about land
it's nothing but parcels of dirt and rock

might as well let everything go
might as well surrender

we've all wanted what we can't have

the land we all came from
already has forgotten us

Dawn

here it comes
through the canopy of leaves

a drizzle of sunlight and rain mix.

Not Geese

Over the mist-trees,
the departing makes their way
past the lake's edge
where sight cannot follow,
trying to beat
fall's inevitable changes.

The departing takes with them
every part of the familiar,
and sound is the last to go.

This wildness, this breathless
parting of life,
death, clouds —

gone.

Where Are You?

I look for you everywhere
until the last light is crimson
setting down casually behind the hills.

I send out my voice into the dark.

My voice returns like an echo,
a great harmful loss.

Where are you?

I keep releasing my voice from my hands,
cadence after cadence,
up into the stars and beyond, hoping
somewhere
you'll hear me.

The Distant Calling

Days come faster, sooner,
like a river of geese over a river,
one reflecting the other, one leaving
while the other cannot travel any further.

I cannot grasp the days.
When I do, they flap crazily like birds
shedding white greasy feathers,
trying to escape.

There is something about leaving
this world behind, and something
about staying —
both are necessary madness.

I feel like I'm about to lose it all —

this world, this imperfect me,
this urge to depart and this call to stay,
this river of silence moving quicker.

I hear the distant calling.

I am holding it back.
My pulse quickens.

Are the geese returning or leaving
or circling
or waiting for me to join?

This Bad Moment

The trees empty themselves —
autumn leaves; red-winged blackbirds;
maple sap; old, twisted, dead branches.

The trees are rustling branches at the wind,
declaring, give me your worst, and I'll withstand it.

Eventually, this bad moment, like the wind, will end.

The Air Trembles with Knowing

details of butterfly bushes
the widening of ferns
the creeping tiny stream

ambient light is the only source
splitting night into absence
and presence

no longer guesswork
but certainty
imagined dangers become familiar

we calm our breathing
into resolve
someone is calling our name

rustling leaves
fireflies descend like a meteor shower
the familiar focuses into shape

In the Dark Violence

I do not feel pain in the sky,
its violent surging of clouds,
magnetically rushing together —
rumbling herds of buffalo. Instead,
I see inexhaustible love
deeply within ourselves,
into a bucket of stillness,
tracing its blue with my fingertips.

Sadness is in the fields,
immense sobs,
rain is filling the trees with depression
disguised as crows.

Clouds are snorting,
pawing at the ground, then
stampede.

Yet in this dark violence,
buttercups, tiny yellow suns,
white beards of Queen Anne's Lace,
tracts of miniature blue Johnny-Jump-Ups
leap for attention.

Unexpected

Part IV

Such Is the Love of the World

An opus is a classical music term for any thematically related composition which can be played together, separately, in order, or out of sequence.

Opus 1

in blur blast haze of high humidity heat
are sizzling insect noises
active in scorch-purge

the insect's happiness is our misery
heat is searing visible like blue flame
angry scar sunburn

dark unknown paths eat scraps of sunlight
waiting to die
bidding their time to claim light

in this startling new worrisome weather
there is little relief
rain shrivels before it arrives

all flash and no substance
not many of us are prepared
for what happens next

Opus 2

in common places
you would expect
soft peaceful things

none of this is ever true

they all experience such fierceness of death
there is no rest

because to close our eyes
is to betray ourselves to violent death
ushering the aftermath
of the wrong kind

do not let anyone tell you differently

no one is protected
not even with prayer

Opus 3

the force that stirs stillness
in water
is not a voice
nor silence opening
flowers in morning
disappearing
as light

absence pushes awe
into the forever

Opus 4

storms will have their way
shadows wave across the lake

a duck skid-lands on the surface
before the storm is unleashed

there is not one moment more deliberate
than a raindrop

there is a certain amount of emptying
to getting to somewhere

it is impossible to see in a deluge

one step then a stumble then
a hillock then a rise over
emptiness

it is a long distance
with no village in sight

this is an uncivilized place

I cannot remember clearly the way back
or if I even knew it to begin with
or if I dreamed this

exotic in its strangeness
almost terrible

and yet
familiar

Opus 5

expediency is not possible

time is turned around and sent back
to the bachelor trees
abandoned by birds of all kinds

kindness is not possible
change is not possible
retribution is not possible

only acceptance

among abandoned miracles
not one moment
takes precedence

a dazed memory
evocating sequences of voices from afar
feeling up close and impersonal

precise words chase the elusive lyric of silence

Opus 6

an unhurried stream over a small rush of rocks
smooths the stones into eggs

listen to trees bud and rasp
in red torrid breath

beware of the inherent danger of hidden things

Opus 7

first love is best love
the winds are carefree women with baskets of white daises

the elegance of the sudden ledge
straight down dizzy
where wet surface
flat shale rock
and spongy moss
make us almost lose footing
like love
reminds me how dangerous it could be
to miss what is in front of us

if we look into the abyss
we will find a longing
calling out to us

Opus 8

rains scour the plains
rub them down
until the earth bone is exposed

lightning splits into flame
brush becomes inflammatory words
incendiary devices

birds collapse out of storms
clasping their wings
what is going on with this wildness

rowers bring their canoes of darkness to shores
step onto the surface tension of loss
nod to each other *let us too ignite*

unspeakable actions call for concentrated silence
blatant disregard become as common
as snapped green branches

Opus 9

when I die
I want to leave behind
more than I have taken

something close to a heartbeat of a hummingbird
with tiny oscillating gossamer wings
tasting poems of memory

and in this instance
speak well of me
say *he had love and loved back equally*

in the loud darkness sing well
like dizzy winds against restless branches
sing

say
he did the best he could
under the circumstances

he tried with his whole heart
murmuring against a gale
across the lake of hopelessness

for this is all I could do
hoping against hope
it was enough

Opus 10

we think the earth is sustainable
it is not

we think given enough time
the world will return to normal
it will not

sustainability will never happen
within our lifetime
there is only so much nature can withstand
before the ecological system collapses

life has limits
yet we see it as endless

there will be a zero point
when we will not be able to return
to the way things were

we have wantonly disregarded
every possible warning

this temperature shift
twenty degrees above normal
is not normal

I remember distantly
when we worried about several generations
beyond what we could see

once we prided ourselves as caretakers
now we seem to pride ourselves
as being careless

we are digging our own graves and do not see it

today in the excruciating heat
begging was heard in the field
and no one was there to hear it

Opus 11

such is the love of a world
laughter is from oceans
a gradual and penetrating light
longed for and found

such is the love of this world
it is like a trust that was promised
before the world began
knowing it would someday be needed

such a love is given
like a mother to a nursing child
while softly singing remembered lullabies
love arrives like heat-flashes

when light is pulled away
stars like so many nervous eyes
remind us of promises our ancestors made
we surely have forgotten

Opus 12

in the green half-shadows
among thick clumps of hawthorn leaves
there is a vapor of people

I know that soon I will join them
I will leave through air
into another place

when light is pulled away
promises our ancestors made
will be challenged or forgotten

Opus 13

a wood thrush always tries to find new sounds
an unexpected improvement
it had my attention
I searched frantically for where it was located

there is a love song in which God is in one note
but we never know which one

I tried to copy every note with full vigor
hoping to find the right one

God would be pleased I had been searching

but it doesn't work that way
it never does

just because a person scatters enough notes
without any understanding of their impact
does not mean we know what they are doing
if a person does not feel the sacredness
of knowing which note it is

God can tell the difference

when it is guesswork
it does not add up

Opus 14

I closed my window
accidentally terminating God's breath

what was I thinking

now I will never know
what I might have heard

I tried to open the window

too late
it was permanently shut

I tried to smash the window with my fist
but my hand broke into spruce pine needles

I tried to run outside
but the stairs kept extending

by the time I ran out of stairs
the street was empty
every house had lifted itself off its foundation
and had followed God

what was I thinking

I had my chance
and I had blown it

the whole neighborhood looked like a tornado hit it
there would be no next time for me
I was dazed when bricks rained on my head

when God's breath entered my window
I should have held onto it
like it was a safety rope with a life preserver

I should have climbed into God's immense pocket

instead
I am left breathless
without God's breath
watching everyone leaving me behind
waving their farewells
going to that better place without me
simply because I did not know
the difference between a cold front and God

all I could do was pant

Wait for me

Opus 15

yellow rain has fallen
heavy as a house suddenly on vast fields
what we do next depends upon too many possibilities
but they are locked in a chest
this is why the world never gets much done

Death has taken all the pretty colors

when someone asks you
Where you are going
in such an incredible hurry
you better be carrying a plank for an ark
focused on how many you can still save

when they roll their eyes thinking you are foolish
you better be putting dark pitch between the cracks
so nothing leaks
watertight is better than swimming lessons

today Death checked once again
to see if I was ready
saw I was busy helping others
noticed later
I was writing in burnishing heat
again later
I was humming a note containing God's smile

Death merely moved on to someone less prepared

Opus 16

it gets dark early
swallowing the final call of sundown

when travelers discover they are nowhere
it is too late
the dark devours them too

I found their trace
a postcard declaring
wish you were here

when I read that
I started packing

that crazy vanishing road
comes to remind us how truly lost we are

we always neglect what matters the most

Opus 17

blackened corpses of stars are going nova
all day it has been crackling with heat insects
I say it is God's voice telling us something important
the heat grinds us for not listening
we cannot seem to leave well enough alone
our futile attempts to improve or streamline life
only make it worse

sheet music passages make wildness
briars and milkweed sends music into trumpets of wind
their melody heals stunted sapling brings light
to darkened air finding cures for emptiness

light
come fill us

heal the forgotten

Opus 18

we are deeply loved yet we don't know it
we do not recognize love in front of us

we are so used to its presence elsewhere
always seeing birds flocking
practicing wider loops
writing love into the sky

we never notice how animals burrow
to get closer to the center
believing God resides *there*

we see God as a hermit
too lonely to see what is going on

Love is never a lost dog shrilling
it is quieter than a leaf forming from a bud

we are so profoundly loved
and we cannot see what is happening
we tear apart hearts like they were paper

when the sunflower tries to copy the sun
no one says
Isn't it miraculous

we are so desperately loved
yet we treat it as flimsy
as ebb tides of cool air

we are so passionately loved
that if God could kiss us
God would

Opus 19

all day a continent of snow tumbled
from the rim of the whitewashed sky
until the ridgeline was erased

nuthatches were shaking the wind
with their song
the violence of snow cannot subdue them

Opus 20

there is a kind of dense fog
smoke screen found in minds

it peels slowly at memory
the kind of forgetfulness of a migrating bird
losing direction
the terminal absence of who we are
until nothing remains of what used to be

pictures of our past
tumble loosely out of the photo album
of our hearts
then loss nibbles
taking every part of passion

I have seen their past shuffling with walkers

some people
all they could do was cry
knowing what was wrong
what was amiss
but unclear
what the heck it could be

Opus 21

there is a precise sizzling
scattered in the lavender fields below
the cedar waxwings
suspended in air like butterfly kites

that sizzling grinds like a person making a key

it is locusts in the heat sweat afternoon
rubbing heavy duty sandpaper
it is voices shattering against the limits of love

the heat has a musty smell
worse than wet fur
or drowned fish
on the sandy edge of a retreating river

God opened a window in the sky
and the world was illuminated
with the same blue of thermal hot springs
and the odd golden shade of their earthen hole

Opus 22

all day has been crackling with heat insects
I say it is God's voice telling us something important
the heat grinds us for not listening

we cannot seem to leave well enough alone
our futile attempts to improve or streamline life
only make it worse

all day our lungs boiled

it is not enough to quit
meddling with things we do not understand

we are the only species going in the opposite direction
dragging along others
unwillingly
into oblivion

we might as well be calling out God

when God finally answers
it won't be pretty

every time I kneel in the garden planting seeds
prayers turning soil over from soured to healthy
the earth is grateful

I can witness to its subtle changes
while others add to its destruction

I'd rather do the tender-touch

A small thing
some would say
yet it is a healing touch
like none other

Opus 23

if God took a branding iron to the sky
would you understand the message

if a warning skimmed across paddling in a canoe
would you look for exemptions in the margins

what would stir it more
what would split open wounds

mistreated people will become tongrass wildflowers
their heads still bent to the ground from shame

where is the justice in that
what is this in the unsettling blur descending

Opus 24

in the thin membrane of a leaf
there is a vein
carrying breath
to the tip of a snag
hundreds of climbing feet above
like a forbidden fruit
on the edge of wind current
like the partial face of God
asking the reason for pollution

one wrong answer
could lead to a rock slide

if I was you
I would start whispering in God's ear

About the Poet

Martin Willitts Jr., an organic gardener and retired librarian who lives in Syracuse, New York, has been an editor for *Comstock Review* and a judge for the New York State Fair Poetry Contest. A gifted and prolific poet, he has garnered numerous awards and publications.

Among his 25 published chapbooks is the the winner of the *Turtle Island Quarterly* Editor's Choice Award, *The Wire Fence Holding Back the World* (Flowstone Press, 2017).

His 15 full-length poetry volumes include the winner of the National Ecological Contest, *Searching For What is Not There* (Hiraeth Press, 2013); and the 2019 Blue Light Press Award Winner, *The Temporary World.*

Numerous other awards include the William K. Hathaway Award, 2013; Bill Holm Witness Poetry Contest, 2013; "Trees" Poetry Contest, 2014; Dylan Thomas International Poetry Contest, 2014; and *Rattle* Ekphrastic Challenge, June 2015.

CPSIA information can be obtained
at www.ICGtesting.com
Printed in the USA
BVHW031802140220
572416BV00001B/10